Dick Whittington

A Victorian Pantomime

Alan Brown

A Samuel French Acting Edition

SAMUELFRENCH-LONDON.CO.UK
SAMUELFRENCH.COM

Copyright © 1987 by Alan Brown
All Rights Reserved

DICK WHITTINGTON is fully protected under the copyright laws of the British Commonwealth, including Canada, the United States of America, and all other countries of the Copyright Union. All rights, including professional and amateur stage productions, recitation, lecturing, public reading, motion picture, radio broadcasting, television and the rights of translation into foreign languages are strictly reserved.

ISBN 978-0-573-06478-4

www.samuelfrench-london.co.uk

www.samuelfrench.com

FOR AMATEUR PRODUCTION ENQUIRIES

UNITED KINGDOM AND WORLD EXCLUDING NORTH AMERICA

plays@SamuelFrench-London.co.uk

020 7255 4302/01

Each title is subject to availability from Samuel French, depending upon country of performance.

CAUTION: Professional and amateur producers are hereby warned that *DICK WHITTINGTON* is subject to a licensing fee. Publication of this play does not imply availability for performance. Both amateurs and professionals considering a production are strongly advised to apply to the appropriate agent before starting rehearsals, advertising, or booking a theatre. A licensing fee must be paid whether the title is presented for charity or gain and whether or not admission is charged.

The professional rights in this play are controlled by Samuel French Ltd, 52 Fitzroy Street, London, W1T 5JR.

No one shall make any changes in this title for the purpose of production. No part of this book may be reproduced, stored in a retrieval system, or transmitted in any form, by any means, now known or yet to be invented, including mechanical, electronic, photocopying, recording, videotaping, or otherwise, without the prior written permission of the publisher. No one shall upload this title, or part of this title, to any social media websites.

The right of Alan Brown to be identified as author of this work has been asserted by him in accordance with Section 77 of the Copyright, Designs and Patents Act 1988

CHARACTERS

Dick Whittington
Tommy, his cat
Alderman Fitzwarren
Alice, his daughter
Emmaline ("**Maggie**"), his cook
Idle Jack, his apprentice
Fairy Bowbells
King Rat
Stage Manager
Urchin Child
Jack Frost
Captain Ginjah
Boatswain
King Neptune
Rustifustican, Sultan of Morocco
Jujube, his daughter
Zeldomphed, his chamberlain
Monkey

Musk Rat
Field Rat
Black Rat
House Rat
Sparks, Mashers, Sailors, Girl-friends, Rats, Customers, Children, Snowflakes, Sunbeams, Fish, Native Guards, Harem Dancers

In the Harlequinade:
Harlequin
Columbine
Pantaloon
Clown
Butcher
Watchman

SYNOPSIS OF SCENES

PART I

SCENE 1	The Land of Fancy
SCENE 2	Cheapside, London—outside Fitzwarren's Shop
SCENE 3	Inside Fitzwarren's Shop
SCENE 4	Highgate Hill
SCENE 5	London Docks

PART II

SCENE 6	The Galley of the *Betsy Jane*
SCENE 7	Neptune's Palace
SCENE 8	The Coast of Morocco
SCENE 9	The Sultan's Palace
SCENE 10	Harlequinade
SCENE 11	The Guildhall, London

MUSICAL NUMBERS

Alan Brown has produced a separate list of song suggestions for use with this pantomime which is available free of charge upon application to Samuel French Ltd. However, please remember that a licence issued by Samuel French to perform this pantomime does NOT include permission to use copyright songs and music. Please read the notice supplied by the Performing Right Society which follows on page vii.

Suggested Incidental and Ballet Music

Page 1	Harlequinade	Fairy Bowbells introduces characters *Jeux d'Enfants*—Bizet, 3, La Poupee (Berceuse) leading into:
Page 1	Harlequinade (cont)	Characters come to life. Butcher woos Columbine. *Jeux d'Enfants*—Bizet, 9, Collin-Maillard (Nocturne) leading into:
Page 1	Harlequinade (cont)	General action, Clown and Harlequin predominantly mischievous *Jeux d'Enfants*—Bizet, 12, Le Bal (Galop)
Page 3		Harlequin is turned into a cat. *The Sleeping Beauty*, Act III, Tchaikovsky. Music for White Cat and Puss in Boots
Page 4		Entrance of Fairy Bowbells, followed by tableau vivant of Dick's meeting with the Cat on the road to London. *Jeux d'Enfants*—Bizet, 1, L'Escarpolette (Reverie)
Page 20	Snow Ballet	Jack Frost summons Wind and Snowflakes to freeze Dick. Snowflakes dance. Fairy Bowbells enters

		with Sunbeams. Snowflakes melt away. Extracts from final section *La Source*—Delibes.
Page 31	Sea Storm	Final movement of storm sequence. 4th movement of *Scheherazade*—Rimsky-Korsakov
Page 33	Fish Ballet	Aquarium from *The Carnival of the Animals*—Saint-Saëns
Page 40	The Sultan's Palace	Harem girls dancing. Maggie plucks her guitar, serenading the Sultan. Extracts from 1st movement of *Scheherazade*
Page 42	Harlequinade	Characters play Blind Man's Buff. *Jeux d'Enfants*, 8, Les Quatre Coins (Esquisse) leading into: Harlequin as Cat *The Sleeping Beauty*, Act III. leading into: Harlequin transformed back from Cat—with Monkey *Jeux d'Enfants*, La Toupie, (Impromtu) to be followed by soft-shoe-shuffle, as per script

SONGS

No 1   Jack and Chorus
No 2   Nurse
No 3   Dick and Alice
No 4   Fitzwarren, Jack, Maggie, Alice and Dick
No 5   Urchin, Jack, Maggie and Dick
No 6   Dick
No 7   Voices
No 8   Captain
No 9   Company
No 10 Company
No 11 Dick, Alice, Fitzwarren, Maggie and Jack
No 12 Jujube
No 13 Rustifustican
No 14 Fitzwarren and Alice
No 15 Rustifustican
No 16 Dick and Company
       Reprise of No. 16, Dick and Company

The following statement concerning the use of music is printed here on behalf of the Performing Right Society Ltd, by whom it was supplied

The permission of the owner of the performing right in copyright music must be obtained before any public performance may be given, whether in conjunction with a play or sketch or otherwise, and this permission is just as necessary for amateur performances as for professional. The majority of copyright musical works (other than oratorios, musical plays and similar dramatico-musical works) are controlled in the British Commonwealth by the PERFORMING RIGHT SOCIETY LTD, 29–33 BERNERS STREET, LONDON W1P 4AA.

The Society's practice is to issue licences authorizing the use of its repertoire to the proprietors of premises at which music is publicly performed, or, alternatively, to the organizers of musical entertainments, but the Society does not require payment of fees by performers as such. Producers or promoters of plays, sketches, etc., at which music is to be performed, during or after the play or sketch, should ascertain whether the premises at which their performances are to be given are covered by a licence issued by the Society, and if they are not, should make application to the Society for particulars as to the fee payable.

PRODUCTION NOTES

In order to preserve a truly Victorian flavour, the Harlequinade is a highly desirable integral ingredient of this pantomime. However, it is by no means indispensable, and there have been several very successful productions by companies of modest resources (professional and amateur) which have omitted the Harlequinade sequences altogether.

During the arrival of the audience an advertisement cloth is displayed bearing 1890s period advertisements by local shops and firms still in existence today.

Immediately prior to the rise of the curtain the advertisement cloth is raised, and a Victorian stage manager comes from behind the curtain with a lighted taper and ignites the (imitation) footlights.

PART I

Scene 1

Fairy Bowbells appears, lit by a single spot

Fairy Welcome girls, and welcome boys!
Now you've left behind your toys.
Join us in adventure time,
And see in this, our Pantomime,
Immortal spirits here at play,
On our Christmas holiday . . .

Music—see page iv

The characters of the Harlequinade are revealed in frozen attitudes. Fairy Bowbells introduces them to the audience:

>WATCHMAN of our happy band,
Keeps the keys of fairyland.
BUTCHER's rich with lots of gold,
But has a heart that's mean and cold;
For one thing only does he pine
The fair and lovely COLUMBINE!
And her father PANTALOON
Says she must marry Butcher soon.
Though some may think he's round the bend,
Old CLOWN's a true and loyal friend.
There's only one he thinks should win
Her hand, that's sprightly HARLEQUIN!
But PANTALOON is far from sure,
For HARLEQUIN is much too poor.
Now watch these spirits on parade
In a gay HARLEQUINADE!

She waves her wand and exits

One by one the characters begin to move. Butcher proposes to Columbine, urged on by Pantaloon. Watchman studies Clown and Harlequin suspiciously, who are the last to move. When they do the action of the Harlequinade becomes very lively, with Harlequin and Clown predominantly mischievous

King Rat enters

King Rat Hold immortals! Cease these antics!
Fruitless are your corybantics.
Kids aren't entertained like that,
Easier to amuse a cat!
What they want is grief and sorrer,
They like lots of blood and horror.
For our evil they will cherish us ...

To the audience, who will be hissing

You shut up you little perishers!!

To the Harlequinade characters

Well may you lot start with fear;
I shall soon be boss round here.
When I'm king of earth and sky
I shall make you squeal and cry.
I shall wipe this kingdom flat!
... Who called me a dirty rat?!!
And when I'm Lord of Land and Sea
You my bonne-bouche bride shall be!

He seizes Columbine

Ah, ha! Ha! Ha! Ha!

Fairy Bowbells enters

Fairy Begone vile Rat! Slink away!
You shall never win the day,
For there's a simple country lad,
Who guards the good, and fights the bad—
"Dick Whittington", with honour true,
Will save mankind from rats like you!

King Rat roars with laughter

King Rat Dick Whittington?—that's really great!
Him I shall soon annihilate.
A simple country lad, you're right!
Why, he's hardly worth the fight.
His career will quickly cease;
I'll swallow him in one big piece.
And when I've tanned that bumpkin's hide,
I'll be back to claim my bride.

King Rat exits, roaring with laughter

Fairy Fear not; for I will guard this land.
He has no magic like my wand.
But his threats in this connection

Part I, Scene 1

> Show that Dick may need protection;
> And if he's to fight a rat,
> What better helpmate than a cat?
> Now who amongst us, sure and quick
> Knows many a crafty feline trick?

The others push forward Harlequin

> Why Harlequin, with magic bat!
> You would make an ideal cat.
> Kneel, receive this magic charm
> To keep Dick Whittington from harm.

She touches Harlequin with her wand. There is a flash, a puff of smoke, and he is changed into a cat. The others gather around to pat and stroke him

> There Harlequin, you are a beauty.
> Farewell now, and do your duty.

Fairy Bowbells exits

A short dance during which the Cat exits amongst fond farewells etc.

A group of Rats enter, who harrass and terrify the Harlequinade characters, and chase them off. The rats acclaim their victory

King Rat enters

King Rat   That's right my faithful rats; I'm pleased—
Yes, very—
To see my subjects in a mood so merry:
It shows my evil schemes succeed.
Musk Rat   You're right!
For evil doing we've an appetite.
King Rat   I'm glad of that, for I your aid require.
Field Rat   Our teeth are always at your service, sire.
King Rat   And that is why, as you'll admit the case is,
In Government you occupy high places.
For be aware my friends, that I have sent
Rats in disguise, even to Parliament!!
But gather round, and I will tell you, rats,
For what I need your further aid.
Rats   Ay, that's
What we all long to hear!
King Rat   It has been fun
For you to ruin Farmer Whittington,
By eating all his grain? . . .

The Rats nod enthusiastically

> . . . And never stopped
> Until his bounteous crops for him you cropped?
> The father, ruined now and quite undone,

	The son, young Dick, his living seeks in London.
	Pursue him thence, and lose no time,
	To drive the lad from poverty to crime!!
Rats	It shall be done!
King Rat	From bad to worse I'll send him!

Fairy Bowbells enters

Fairy	Oh no you won't, for I mean to befriend him.
King Rat	What! You ... again!!
House Rat	It's Bowbells!
Musk Rat	Queen of Cats!
Field Rat	She's just a fairy!
Fairy	But I'm rough on rats!
	A faithful cat I've sent Dick to attend him,
	And from your machinations to defend him.
King Rat	This cat tale is a fairy tale she's told.
Fairy	You doubt my word?
All Rats	We do!
Fairy	Then just behold! ...

Through the gauze backing we see Dick Whittington on his way to London. He is very weary, and sits on a milestone bearing the inscription: "(local town)" A LONG WAY", and "LONDON—FURTHER STILL". From his pack he takes some bread, which he starts to eat

The Cat enters, and rubs his head against Dick's leg

Dick gives him some bread. The Cat indicates: "Are you going to London?" Dick nods. Cat indicates that he is going too. They shake hands, and move off together

The Lights behind the gauze fade

	That cat, Dick Whittington, where'er he goes,
	With my aid shall protect from all his foes.
King Rat	Your aid indeed! Your boasting you'll regret.
Fairy	Dick's cat will cause you lots of worry yet.
House Rat	She really means it!
Fairy	Yes, without a doubt
King Rat	Oh! then you'll find you've got your work cut out.
Fairy	I'll do my best to worst you.
King Rat	Fire away.
	I'll do my worst to best you, I may say.
Fairy	Your worst at best will be of small account.
King Rat	At best your worst to much will not amount.
Fairy	A truce to words, and let the fight begin.
King Rat	'Tis good 'gainst evil.
Fairy	Yes, and good will win.

All exit

Scene 2

Outside Alderman Fitzwarren's Store, London
Young Sparks and Mashers are parading with their Girl-friends

Song 1

Everyone sings the first verse

Idle Jack enters to sing the second verse

The Stage Manager wheels on the words of the chorus on an easel, then exits

Everyone, including the audience, sing the chorus. Jack sings the next verse and everyone finishes off with the chorus

Alderman Fitzwarren appears at a window

Fitzwarren Hey you! Buzz off! Go on! Getoffahtofit!

All exit

Fitzwarren comes onstage

    A pretty thing at this time of the morning,
    Singing and dancing, people's slumbers scorning.
    As I'm an alderman of London Town,
    I won't put up with it, I'll put it down.
    The shutters not yet off! Where is that lazy
    Idle apprentice? He will drive me crazy!
    You lie-a-bed, come out here with agility.
    There is no limit to his lie-ability.
    Come, set about your work, sir, double quick,
    Or I shall set about you with a stick. (*Shouting*)
    Jack! Jack, you knave, your ugly carcass show,
    Where is Jack Idle, I would like to know.
    AH!

He finds Jack. And pulls him on by one ear

Jack If you that way hollo, guv'nor, I should say
You'll wake the people up in Holloway.
I've been up all night!
Fitzwarren What's that you said? Been up all night???
Jack Yes, sir, upstairs in bed!
Fitzwarren Watch your tongue!
Jack (*squinting*) I can't my nose is in the way!
(*Pointing out into the audience*) Oooh, look! Beans!!
Fitzwarren Haricot Beans?
Jack No—Human Be'ans!
Fitzwarren I don't wish to know that. Now listen! ...
The night before last you came home yesterday,

	You came home this morning, last night, If today you come home tomorrow— You're not sleeping in this house tonight!
Jack	But——
Fitzwarren	Silence! And what about those shutters?
Jack	Fitzwarren to young Jack did utter "Go my boy and shut the shutter!" "The shutter's shut!" young Jack did utter, "I cannot shut it any shutter!"
Fitzwarren	They should be open, lazy, idle Jack! Now you shall feel my cane upon your back!

He chases Jack off

There is a loud explosion from inside the house. Maggie, the cook, runs out bearing a large burning black pie. She crosses to the pump and pours water on the pie, which she then drops on to a table outside Fitzwarren's shop. The table breaks in two and collapses. She turns, and sees the audience ... (musical background)

Maggie Ooh, hello!
I'm Fitzy's cook, and I can proudly boast
I boss the show—that is—I rule the roast!
I'd leave this place tomorrow, but you see
Fitz's apprentice, Jack is mashed on me!

... Anyway, who have we got in tonight? (*She peers into the auditorium and finds a child*) Hello, there's a pretty little girl down there. What's your name, love? ... That's a lovely name! And where do you come from? ... Oh, yes. That'll be a nice place when it's finished! How old are you? ... And are you married yet? ... No?? You don't want to be left on the shelf, you know. Have you started your bottom drawer yet? ... No??! Here, we'll need to get you gingered up. Now let's see. Who have we got over here? (*She peers into the auditorium on the other side of the house*) I say! Here's a handsome young man down here. (*To little boy*) What's your name, love? ... Where do you come from? ... Oh, well, you could always move! (*or local gag, in period*) ... And how old are you? ... !!! (*To little girl*) I've got just the man for you, duck! Catch 'em when they're young! And he must have a bob or two, sitting in the posh seats up the front here. (*To boy*) Now, here's what you do young (*boy's name*). During the interval you go and meet young (*girl's name*) and then you can buy her a great big ice-cream, and lots of sweets, and flowers, and a yacht on the Riviera. Will you do that? ... No? What do you mean "No"? Isn't that a typical man! Oh, never mind. Perhaps he's poor. Are you poor, love? I know what it's like to be poor. You know, when we were kids we were so poor mummy couldn't afford to buy me shoes. Do you know what she used to do? She used to paint me feet black and lace up me toes! And of course, nowadays, I can't expect anything better. Not at my time of life! ... (*She sings*)

Part I, Scene 2   7

Song 2

(*Speaking*) Oh! Look at the state of that pie! Talk about a burnt offering. It's this new gas supply, you know. It's up one minute and down the next, like a pint o' stout. And me with a wedding-breakfast to serve before the end of the show ... I'll tell you what! Would *you* help me, children? Would you? I'll just get me oven, then I'll tell you what to do. Mr ——! Will you bring me oven on, please?

The Stage Manager wheels on a Victorian gas-stove, with a large turkey on the top

The boys and girls are going to help me to cook the turkey. Now, I'll put the turkey in the oven. There! Turn on the gas. Light it ... Now! If that starts to smoke, I want you all to yell out; "MAGGIE!!!" Will you do that? Come on, let's have a try. After three—one, two, two and half—three!

Audience Maggie!

Maggie Oh, come on! You can do better than that ... etc.

As she speaks the stove gives off a puff of smoke

Audience Maggie!

Maggie looks into the oven, gives the thumbs up signal closes the oven door, and adjusts the gas knob

Maggie That's fine! Now I don't have to worry if the gas goes up or down, I'm so looking forward to that wedding breakfast, Oh, I'm that grateful children ...

The stove gives off a puff of smoke

Audience Maggie!

Maggie looks into the oven as before

Maggie Och, that's grand! Grand!

Idle Jack enters

Jack	What's all the row, Cookie?
Maggie	Cookie!!!
Jack	Don't be angry, it sounds like fun!
Maggie	Cookie! Indeed for cheek you tak' the bun!
Jack	(*aside*)
	I makes the old girl think I loves her. Why?
	A'cos she gives me puddin', cake, and pie.
	I love the guv'nor's daughter. She, alas,
	Alack! rejects me for a lack of brass.

He puts his arm round Maggie's waist

Come, don't be cross, I didn't mean to vex.
So pray forgive me, fairest of your sex!

Maggie	You think me beautiful, sweet youth?
Jack	Beautiful's not the word. (*Aside*) And that's the truth!
Maggie	Jack—you may—kiss me.
Jack	(*looking disgusted*) What? No thanks, my pet! You see I've not been vaccinated yet!

Maggie grabs Jack into her arms. The stove gives off a puff of smoke

Audience Maggie!

Maggie drops Jack and attends to the stove

Fitzwarren enters

Fitzwarren	What's all this noise?—And no-one in the shop! Each hoppertunity away you hop, Leaving the counter and my wares behind.
Jack	Counter attractions out of doors we find.
Fitzwarren	Is it for this I give you board?
Jack	Don't keep on. The only board we get is what we sleep on. We want our wages, guv'nor!
Fitzwarren	Well, my man Just keep on wanting 'em as long's you can. My "Bankrupt Stock" Sale bankrupt left me nearly, My "Clearance" Sale cleared *me* out very clearly. I'm ruined!
Jack	A happy thought!
Fitzwarren	(*eagerly*) What can it be?
Jack	Give Cook away with half-a-pound of tea!

Maggie (*lovingly to Jack*) You couldn't give your little Maggie away with half-a-pound of tea, could you Jack?

Jack That's true. We'd have to make it at least a pound of tea!

Maggie takes a swipe at Jack who ducks, and she hits Fitzwarren

Maggie	That was a mistake, sir. It's Jack's to blame! (*Aside*) Silly old fool!
Fitzwarren	(*aside*) Infuriating Dame! (*Aloud*) Come, come now—bustle!
Maggie (*indignantly*)	Sir?
Fitzwarren	I don't mean you! Let's get indoors, there is a lot to do.
Jack	(*as they exit*) A lot to do! It's nonsense that he speaks, We haven't done a customer for weeks!

They all exit into the shop

Dich Whittington enters with Cat

Dick	So, this is London, whose streets I've been told, Lead on to fortune, and are paved with gold!

Part I, Scene 2

>Alas! How many, seeking wealth and fame
>They've led ere now to poverty and shame!
>Streets paved with gold forsooth! Oh what a whopper!
>As yet, I've not picked up a single copper.
>I've tried to get work, there's no denying.
>Tried, yes, but failed!

Cat rubs against him

>Ah, Tom, this life is trying,
>I feel, old friend, to you I will confess,
>Alone within this peopled wilderness.
>"Fitzwarren, Merchant", Tom, I'll have a shy here.
>Here goes!

Before he can knock on the door, Alice Fitzwarren emerges

	(*Aside*) How pretty!
Alice	(*aside*) What a handsome peasant!
Dick	Do you require a young man, miss, at present?
Alice	Oh, sir! (*Aside*) He's very nice!
Dick	I mean——
Alice	Just so, But pa says I'm too young to have a beau.
Dick	I meant a shop lad, miss!
Alice	(*disappointed*) Oh! Did you?
Dick	Rather!
Alice	Then in that case, you'd better ask my father. Oh! What a splendid fellow!
Dick	(*aside*) Hark at that! (*Aloud*) Thanks miss!
Alice	I don't mean you. I mean the cat. Who's can he be?
Dick	He's mine, miss, though I'm poor.
Alice	Is he a tabby cat?
Dick	Yes, tabby sure.
Alice	(*aside*) He is a nice young man. Somehow or other I seem to like him better than a brother.
Dick	What strange sensation's this I labour under?
Alice	Is it a case of love at sight I wonder?
Dick	Nay, never doubt it. Say but that you'll be My little sweetheart, and I'll love but thee.
Alice	A sweetheart. What is that?
Dick	He is sweet miss, The boy who's privileged to go like this (*He kisses her*) And also that! (*He kisses her*) I hope I make it plain?
Alice	Oh, please do tell it me all o'er again!

Song 3

A duet by Dick and Alice with the Stage Manager entering as before with the words so the audience can join in the chorus

A puff of smoke from the oven

Audience Maggie!

Maggie enters, and sees to the stove with a thumbs-up sign to the audience. She is followed on by Fitzwarren and Jack

Fitzwarren	Hullo, hullo! Who *are* you, you young scamp?
Dick	A poor lad out of work, sir.
Fitzwarren	Oh! a tramp!
Dick	I'm seeking work.
Maggie	A farthing, I could bet it, He's seeking work, and hoping not to get it.
Dick	Up from the country, sir, without misgiving, I've tramped to London Town to earn a living, But work seems scarce, the outlook's far from pleasant.
Alice	There are too many out of work at present. Give him a situation, Pa.
Dick	Please do.
Maggie	Don't be a fool, man, or this day you'll rue.
Dick	Is it a crime to have an empty purse?
Jack	A crime? Society knows nothing worse.
Alice	Give him a chance, Pa; let the poor lad stop.
Fitzwarren	Well, if you don't object to sweep the shop.
Maggie	And black the shoes.
Jack	And also clean the winders.
Fitzwarren	Kindle the fires.
Maggie	And carry out the cinders.
Fitzwarren	Run errands.
Jack	And sit up for me.
Alice	He won't!
Jack	Oho! I'll make him sit up if he don't.
Fitzwarren	In short, you'll have to do what each one wishes,
Maggie	And turn the spit for me, and wash the dishes.
Dick	And pray what are the wages?
Fitzwarren	Wages? Zounds! You'll pay a premium of twenty pounds.
Dick	I haven't got it!
Fitzwarren	What?!
Alice	Pa, rage don't foster.
Fitzwarren	Hasn't got twenty pounds——
Jack	Oh, he's an imposter.
Maggie	Of what you've got, boy, give the boss a hint.
Dick	I've got a penny and a peppermint.
Maggie	In other words he's skint!

Part I, Scene 2

Alice	Papa, you know there's always satisfaction
	In doing——
Fitzwarren	Customers——
Alice	A kindly action.
	Engage this lad, then, without more delay.
Dick	Oh, hasn't she a most engaging way!
Fitzwarren	I will—and pay him wages—don't be vexed—
	Nothing first year, and double that the next.
Maggie	And you'll be expected, young man, to invest yer savings in the business.

Song 4

Fitzwarren, Maggie and Jack sing Song 4 which includes a dance

Dick	Oh, thank you sir, and you miss, for assistance.
Jack	Just thank the lady at a proper distance.
Fitzwarren	And now your name boy? If a name you've got.
Dick	'Tis Richard Whittington.
Fitzwarren	Eh? Richard what-Ington?
Dick	No; Whittington. Folks call me Dick.
	For short, please sir——
Jack	(*mimicking*) "Please sir!"—He makes me sick.
Alice	Oh I like "Dick!"
Fitzwarren	Then "Dick" it is, agreed.
Jack	She "likes" Dick, does she? (*Aside*) Then I'll have his bleed!

Jack makes to kick Dick, but is bitten by the cat

Cat	Meeow-ow-ow! Phitz!
Jack	Murder!
Fitzwarren	What was that?
Dick	Only a "Harmless necessary cat!"
Jack	It bit me in the leg, the imbecile!
Alice	I hope it doesn't make the poor cat ill!
Fitzwarren	Whose cat is it?
Alice	'Tis Dick's, and ain't he nice?
Dick	Just give hiM 'ouse room, and he'll CATch your mice.
	Give him the tip, and quickly he'll extermin-
	Ate your rats, and other kinds of vermin!

Maggie (*beginning to sneeze*) Ah—ah—ee-ooh-ah ... tchoo! Oh, the beast! I can't bear cats! They make me ... ah-ooh-ah-oh ... they make me ... Oooahtchooo! ... sneeze!! Take it away! Take it away! Shoo! Shoo!
Alice Oh, no! He's a dear little cat. He only wants to be friendly.
Maggie He's a horrible cat! All cats are horrible. Aaahtchoo!
Alice I know! Maybe the boys and girls will help. Look, boys and girls, will

you help Maggie? Every time she sneezes, will you say "Bless you!" Will you? I'm sure it would make her feel better. Come on, let's try!
Maggie Aaahtchooo!!
All Bless you!
Alice Oh, I don't think she heard that properly, did you Maggie?
Maggie No, me ears seem to be all bunged up!
Alice Let's try it again. Come on kids. Mums and dads too. "Bless you!" — every time she sneezes . . .
Maggie Aaaatchooo!!
All Bless you!
Maggie Aaaatchooo!!
All Bless you!
Alice There. Does that make you feel better?
Maggie Oooh, much better. Thank you children, very much. You've no idea what a difference that makes. Aaatchoo!
All Bless you!
Alice Papa, may I now keep the cat?
Fitzwarren My child, You shall do so.
Dick Oh, thanks!
Maggie (*aside*) With rage I'm wild!
Jack (*aside*) With jealousy my heart is madly thumping!
Maggie (*aside*) I see! I see the way the cat is jumping! Aaaatchooo!!
All Bless you!
Dick (*to Alice*) You are a trump!
Alice I think I've won the trick.
Maggie ⎱
Jack ⎰ (*together, aside*) For this we'll be revenged on Master Dick!

They all repeat the chorus of Song 4

All exit

SCENE 3

Inside Alderman Fitzwarren's Shop

Rats are everywhere, devouring the last of some food left on the counter

The Cat enters and chases the Rats away

One Rat returns and approaches Maggie's stove

It gives off a puff of smoke. The audience shouts "Maggie!"

The Rat scampers off

Maggie enters, followed by Jack, attends to the oven, and gives the thumbs-up signal

Maggie	Well Jack, how is the new apprentice doin'?
Jack	He'll do for us! I mean he'll be our ruin.
	He's far too diligent, the artful pup,
	Does so much work, Cook, that he shows me up.
Maggie	Well Jack, me deary, we must hatch some plot
	To make it for this cool young shaver hot.
Jack	I have! I have! I've hatched the plot I mean.
	I sneaked old Fitz's purse, by all unseen,
	And in Dick's pocket placed it!
Maggie	I'm amused,
	Dick of the theft of course will be accused!
	It's a grand joke!
Jack	I think I've done it pat,
	And now the next thing is I'll kill that cat!
Maggie	The next thing is the dinner to prepare.
	We'll have hare soup today.
Jack	Hare! Hare!
Maggie	Where's the meat gone?
Jack	That cat!
Maggie	The little thief!
	We can't have beef-steak pie without the beef!
Jack	You mean the meat's all gone?
Maggie	Even the fat!
	He's gone and wolfed the lot.
Jack	I'll kill that cat!

Dick and Cat enter

Maggie	(*to Cat*) Aaahtchooo!!!
Audience	Bless you!
Maggie	Just come and turn the spit, you thievin' chit yer!
	Don't spit your spits at me now, or I'll spit yer!

She sends Cat off

	Aaahtchooo!
Audience	Bless you!
Jack	You get to work, you sulky beggar brat,
	Or else I'll——
Dick	(*squaring to him*) What?
Jack	I'll kill that cat!
	'Ere! Can you fight young fellow?
Dick	Fight? Well rather!
	Why do you ask?
Jack	Because ... so can ... me father!

Fitzwarren enters

Fitzwarren Have you sanded the floor?
Dick Yes, sir!
Fitzwarren Mixed the flour for the puddings?

Maggie Yes, sir!
Fitzwarren And finished blending the whisky?
Jack Yes sir, I've finished the whisky!
Fitzwarren Then get out the merchandise.

He exits

They prepare the shop for customers, Maggie and Jack behind the counter, Dick behind the cash-till. The shop door opens and the bell rings. All three shout "Shop!"

A child enters

Maggie (*all smiles*) And what can I do for you?
Child A penn'orth of aniseed balls, please.
Maggie (*face falls*) Oh! Aniseed balls! A penn'orth. Right!

The aniseed balls are on the very highest shelf. Maggie is obliged to get a ladder, climb up, get the jar, descend, put a fistful into a bag, hand them over to the child ...

There you are. A penn'orth of aniseed balls! Pay at the desk!

Maggie ascends the ladder to replace the jar

A customer enters, the bell rings

All shout "Shop". The Child gives a penny to Dick who puts it into the cash-till

The child exits

Customer A pair of blue braces, please.
Jack Blue braces?
Customer Blue braces.
Jack That's funny, my brother always wears pink braces!
Customer Pink braces?
Jack Pink braces. Do you know why?
Customer No?
Jack To keep his trousers up! (*He disappears behind the counter*)
Customer (*to Maggie, who has just descended from returning the jar*) And a penn'orth of aniseed balls, please.
Maggie Aniseed balls? Are you sure? (*She indicates items on the counter*) We have some beautiful bullseyes. Gorgeous gobstoppers. Fascinating humbugs.
Customer No. Aniseed balls, please.
Maggie Aniseed—balls. (*She ascends the ladder, and repeats the business*)
Jack (*appearing*) There you are, sir. Blue braces—finest quality! (*He stretches them and releases one end, hitting Maggie, who is on the ladder, in the behind*) Anything else, sir?
Customer Just the aniseed balls.
Jack Just the aniseed balls, Maggie.
Maggie All right! All right! (*She descends*) There you are, a penn'orth of aniseed balls. Pay at the desk! (*She ascends the ladder to replace the jar*)

Part I, Scene 3
15

A 2nd child enters. They all shout "Shop!"

The Customer pays Dick and exits

(As she comes off the ladder) Yes?
2nd Child A penn'orth of aniseed balls, please.
Maggie Aniseed balls? Wouldn't you rather have a couple of gobstoppers? Or a bottle of gin?
2nd Child *(starting to howl)* No! No! I want a penn'orth of aniseed balls!!!
Maggie All right!! Allrightallrightallrightallright!! ... Aniseed balls! *(Up she goes again)*

2nd Customer enters

They all shout "Shop!". The Customer rushes quickly over to Jack

2nd Customer Quick! Quick! Have you got something good for a terrible pain in the head?
Jack A pain in the head? The very thing, sir. Sharp-pointed aspirins!
2nd Customer Sharp-pointed aspirins? What are they for?
Jack Splitting headaches. Pay at the desk!

The 2nd Customer pays Dick and rushes out

A 3rd Child enters

They all shout "Shop!"

Maggie *(descending, to 2nd Child)* There you are, a penn'orth of aniseed balls. Play at the desk.

2nd Child does so, and exits

(To 3rd Child) Now then! *Before* I put this jar back do *you* want a penn'orth of aniseed balls?
3rd Child No, I don't.
Maggie Right! Thank heavens for that! *(She climbs the ladder replaces the jar, descends, and confronts the child)* Now then, me duck, what do you want?
3rd Child *Two* penn'orth of aniseed balls, please!
Maggie *(weeping)* Oh! oohooo! Oohoooo! *(She ascends)*

A drunk enters, and staggers across to Jack

All shout "Shop!"

Drunk Give us a bottle of whisky!
Jack Bottle of whisky? Certainly! There you are!
Drunk No, I've changed me mind. I'll have a bottle of gin instead. Can I change it?
Jack Certainly, certainly. *(He exchanges the whisky for gin)* That'll be five shillings.
Drunk What will?
Jack The gin.
Drunk But I changed it — for the whisky!

Jack But you didn't pay for the whisky!
Drunk Well I didn't take the whisky!
Jack Oh yes that's right. (*But he has doubts*)

The drunk exits with the bottle of gin

Maggie (*just back*) TWO penn'orth of aniseed balls!
Maggie ⎫
Jack ⎭ (*together*) Pay at the desk!
3rd Child Thank you!

The Child pays Dick and exits

Maggie collapses exhausted over the counter

An Urchin-girl, head covered with shawl, etc. enters with the bottle of gin and crosses timidly to Jack

As she enters, all shout "Shop!"

Jack And what do you want?

Song 5

Song 5 is for Urchin and a close harmony quartet

During the song we see through the gauze, a tableau-vivant of "The Drunkard's Home"—Drunkard at table with empty bottle gazes trauma-like into the audience, wife stands with head in her hands—weeping, ragged children without shoes sit about also weeping; Policeman stands in the background, Bailiff stands beside Drunkard with eviction order, etc., etc. . . . as they sing, Maggie and Jack still clutch a bottle of whisky and a bottle of gin respectively . . .

Urchin 'Ere! *Mum* says will you change it?
Maggie (*sobbing*) Of course, of course. What for?
Urchin (*snatching the bottle from Maggie*) A bottle of whisky. She can't stand gin.

She exits

Fitzwarren and Alice enter

Fitzwarren (*as he enters*) Now then, now then! What's going on here? (*To Maggie*) What are *you* doing?
Maggie Nothing!
Fitzwarren (*to Jack*) And what are *you* doing?
Jack Helping *her*!
Fitzwarren Well you three are a fine pair if I ever saw one! What's that bottle? (*Pointing at Jack, asking Dick*)
Dick Gin, sir.
Fitzwarren Who gave you that?
Jack Oh please sir it was Dick. (*Aside*) I'll kill that cat!
Fitzwarren (*snatching gin from Jack*) You greedy Varlet! But I'll make you rue it!

Part I, Scene 3

Dick	It wasn't I sir!
Maggie	Oooooh! I saw you do it! I don't believe he's honest.
Alice	That's not true!
Fitzwarren	Now Alice, this has naught with you to do.
Alice	Our troth is plighted.
Maggie	Then it's a fearful plight!
Fitzwarren	My daughter with a common 'prentice mooning?
Jack	I've often seen 'em in the corners spooning!
Dick	I love Miss Alice.
Alice	Dick, whate'er they do, Your loving sweetheart ever will be true.
Fitzwarren	You love this pauper?
Alice	Yes.
Maggie	The cheeky lass!
Dick	You are a girl of metal, Alice.
Maggie	. . . Brass!
Dick	Love levels all, you know.
Jack	That's very true.
Maggie	Just hold your jaw now, or I'll level you.
Fitzwarren	From my establishment begone!
Maggie	Away and pack Yer carpet bag.
Alice	Oh, Dick!
Jack	That means the sack!
Alice	Give him some money, Pa. You can't do any less.
Fitzwarren	Well, here's a copper, boy; you shan't go penniless. My purse is gone!
Jack	Dick took it!
Dick	That's not true, The one who stole the guv'nor's purse was you! I saw you Jack.
Jack	This is a plot I say To take an orphan's character away. 'Ere search me if you like.
Fitzwarren	I'll first search Dick. I won't be taken in by such a trick.
Maggie / **Jack**	(*together*) Shame! Shame!!
Alice	To search my Dick you'd never dare!
Dick	Fear nothing, I am innocent, I swear.
Fitzwarren	The purse is here!
Maggie	Then Dick's a thief, that's flat.
Jack	Call in the p'lice, and then I'll kill that cat!

Tommy enters

Maggie	Aaahtchooo!
Audience	Bless you!

Fitzwarren	This is your gratitude!
Jack	(*to Dick*) You'd better hook it.
Alice	I don't believe, Papa, that Richard took it.
Dick	I care not for their wicked spite and malice, While you believe me innocent, Miss Alice.
Fitzwarren	Be off!
Dick	Farewell.
Alice	Our love they cannot sever, I'm thine alone.
Dick	And I am thine forever.

Dick exits with the Cat

Music, as Alice reprises a verse of Song 3

Alice weeps bitterly

Scene 4

Highgate Hill, with a view of London

Bells are ringing in the distance, as Dick and Cat enter

Dick	Well, Tom, we've turned our backs on London now, And won't turn back again, old boy.
Cat	More-ow!
Dick	The lights of London showed us some sad sights. Poor Tom's delighted when I mention "lights". Like me you've had your share of kicks and cuffs, Your lights are few, but many your rebuffs. Hark to Bow Bells! How merrily they chime. They seem to speak to me, Tom, of a time, When I'll be rich and great. The thought is pleasant. A penny's all my riches just at present.

He reads the milestone

Four miles to London! We'll not go back there,
For London's a delusion and a snare,
To those devoid of cash. Ah Tom, it's sad,
To be an outcast, friendless, little lad.
No father's care, no mother's sweet caress,
No heart-felt prayer your young career to bless.
These are the things make life and living worth,
But poor Dick hasn't got a friend on earth.

Cat business

	Forgive me Tom! *Your* friendship, I'll not doubt it.
Cat	More-ow!
Dick	All right, make no more row about it!

Part I, Scene 4

Cat More-ow!

Tom indicates the audience

Dick What's that, Tom? You think I've made some pals out there too? Well, maybe you're right Tommy! (*To the audience*) Are you my pals? ... Tell you what—if you are—like Tommy says—why don't we try something ... Every time I shout out "Hiya kids!"—You shout out "Hiya Dick!" Then, no matter what happens, I shan't feel so lonely. All right, let's try it—Hiya kids!
Audience Hiya Dick!
Dick Oh come on now, you can do better than that! ... *etc*. Hiya kids!
Audience Hiya Dick!
Dick Hiya, kids!
Audience Hiya Dick!

Song 6

Dick sings Song 6 with the audience joining in the chorus as the Stage Manager wheels in the words

Dick Hiya kids!
Audience Hiya Dick!
Dick   Your kindness, Tommy, recognition merits,
While I've Old Tom, I shan't be out of spirits.
Hullo, boy, here's a bank. I think the dodge
For us to try, is on this bank to lodge.
Why, it's a clover bank. Now just give over,
Tonight, at any rate, we'll be in clover.
Cosy in Tommy, all our warmth to keep,
And now for Nature's sweet restorer, sleep.

They sleep

King Rat enters

King Rat   What, feeling cold? Your doom is set!
Believe me, you've felt nothing yet.
I'll finish you whate'er the cost;
I'll call upon my friend, Jack Frost.
Jack Frost! Jack Frost! What, are you there?
Do come and *freeze* this stupid pair!

The sound of hissing and the crash of cymbals

Jack Frost appears. The Lights turn hard and cold

   Ah! Come my friend! You see these two?
I think you know what you must do.
A chilly death, that's far from nice,
Turn them to a block of ice.
Make the cold north wind to blow,
And bury them beneath the snow!

Snow Ballet (Music—see page vi)

Jack Frost summons up wind and snow. The sound of an icy wind rises. Snow-lighting-effect begins

"Snowflakes" enter, and dance with Jack Frost around Dick and Tom. They cover with snow the bodies—of Dick and Tommy

Fairy Bowbells enters

Fairy   Jack Frost!!! It seems I'm just in time.
You shan't commit this wicked crime.
With golden beams the sun shall flood.

She waves her wand

And warm their cold, congealing blood.

Sunbeams enter, dancing

Sunshine begins to warm the stage, and a rosy dawn glows from one side. Dawn music. Birdsong. Jack Frost cringes with fear

I see, Jack Frost, my magic's felt.
Be off now, quickly, ere you melt!

Jack Frost and winter "elements" flee in terror

(*To King Rat*)

What feebleness you demonstrate.
Again your evil I frustrate.
Be gone! Don't try another trick.
You'll never learn to conquer Dick!

King Rat   In different elements I'll meet you,
Next time with *victory* to greet you!!!!

He snarls and exits

Fairy   Sleep on, Dick Whittington, and calmly dream
Of future days that all too happy seem
Ring out, ye Fairy Bells of Bow, once more,
And tell him of his wealth and fame in store.
Tho' black your waking outlook, don't despair,
Thou shalt, of London, be three times Lord Mayor.
Peal out, ye merry bells, a sweet refrain,
Bidding our sleeping hero, "Turn again".

Fairy Bowbells exits

Dick and Tom awaken

Dick   'Twas but a dream then? Puss, I could have sworn
That on the air a pleasant voice was borne,
Which bade me "turn again", and not despair,
And promised I should thrice be made Lord Mayor.

Part I, Scene 5

'Twas but a cruel fantasy, I know,
And yet—what say the chiming Bells of Bow?
Hark to them Tom—they seem to say quite plain,
"Turn again, Whittington, turn, turn again!"

Over the bells, voices are heard singing a round based on the traditional air: "Turn Again, Whittington"

Song 7

Voices (*off*)
Ding dong, ding dong!
Ding dong, ding dong!

Turn again Whittington,
Thou worthy citizen,
Lord Mayor of London.

Turn again Whittington,
London's Lord Mayor!
London's Lord Mayor!

Dick
Oh Tommy, how to act I'm at a loss.
My penny! That's it! We'll have a toss.
We stay, if heads; go back, if tails should fall.
Fire away, Tommy, you shall have the call.
What do you say?

Tommy holds up his tail

Oh, tails! ... And you are right!
So come along! The world I'll boldly fight.
If others go abroad, why shouldn't I,
In foreign lands, to seek my fortune, try?
Though fate should frown again, I won't despair,
My aim and object—London's civic chair!

He marches off, followed by Tommy, who marches behind him, in step

Voices (*off; crescendo*) London's Lord Mayor! London's Lord Mayor!

The bells swell in a crescendo

Scene 5

London Docks

The "Betsy Jane" is alongside. Beside a barrel on which is a book for signing on, is a notice: "Ship's Crew Wanted—Sign Here". Another sign further off reads: "Trips round the harbour. Married men 6d. Wives thrown in"

The Captain and the Boatswain enter, carrying a large crate

Captain Phew! It's lighter when you put it down.
Boatswain Ooh! I don't feel well!
Captain Don't feel well? How's your appetite?
Boatswain Eat like a horse.
Captain Sleep all right?
Boatswain Like a dog!
Captain You'd better see the vet.

The Boatswain exits

Song 8

The Captain sings Song 8

The Stage Manager enters with the chorus words so the audience can join in

King Rat enters, with attendant Rats wearing sailors' hats

King Rat	Ahhhhhhhhh!
	They told me I would find you here.
	Turn right they said, straight down the pier.
	I know you're looking for a crew;
	There's four lads here I think would do.
	You see? They've even got their hats!
Captain	But 'arf a mo'—they look like——
King Rat	Careful!!
	They're very bright, and how they work!
	Whate'er the task, they never shirk.
	Now sign the book lads, then go to it.
	Believe me Captain, you won't rue it.

The Rats squeak with delight, and sign the book, then run back to King Rat, still squeaking ...

Captain (*during the above*) Well, as a favour to you. But they're a bit odd-looking you know! (*He inspects their signatures curiously*)

King Rat	Now darlings mine, you know our ruse
	To terminate their silly cruise.
	Get it?
Rats	Got it!
King Rat	Good!
	When once at sea I'll start a gale
	To snap their mast and rip their sail
	Get it?
Rats	Got it!
King Rat	Good!
	Through the ship's keel you must gnaw,
	Then down she'll sink, to be no more.
	Get it?
Rats	Got it!
King Rat	Good!
	Now climb aboard that sad old barge.

Part I, Scene 5

	Goodbye, my darlings! *Bon voyage!*
	Get 'em?
Rats	(*delightedly*) Got 'em!!
King Rat	(*triumphantly*) Good!!!

The Rats board the "Betsy Jane", squeaking happily. King Rat exits, chuckling gleefully

Dick enters with Cat

Dick Hiya kids!
Audience Hiya Dick!

Dick	I've reached the docks at last, but haven't found A berth on board a vessel outward bound.

The Boatswain enters

	I beg your pardon, but——
Boatswain	Hello, my nipper! What do you want?
Dick	I want to see the skipper.
Captain	Well, young 'un, just look here, and I've a notion You'll see the handsomest as sails the ocean.
Dick	I want to sail it with you.
Boatswain	Oh, I sees!
Captain	Been afloat before, sir?
Dick	If, you please, Experience in sailing I don't lack, I've sailed from (*) to (*) and back!
Boatswain	Are you an ordinary seaman?
Dick	Eh?
Captain	He's an extra-ordinary one, I'd say! Have you a weather eye?
Dick	(*aside*) May I be shot, If I know whether I have or not! (*Aloud*) Yes!
Captain	Dance a hornpipe?
Dick	Yes.
Boatswain	Well that's good noos. But can yer chaw terbaccer?
Dick	When I choose. Am I engaged?
Captain	Of course you are.
Dick	Oh, joy!
Captain	You'll make a very handsome cabin boy.
Boatswain	Hullo, young fellow, just mind what you're at; We sailors take objection to the "cat"!
Dick	He's rough on rats! No dog can kill 'em neater; And then besides, he's such a feline creature!

---

*Locations on local river—the more ridiculous the better

Captain	He'll kill the rats, you say?
Dick	Yes, with celerity.
Captain	This puss may be a wonder to pussterity. Take him aboard. Becalmed we cannot be, So long's we're sure of "cat's-paws" on the sea.

All exit

The stove gives off a puff of smoke, the audience shout "Maggie!"

Maggie enters, followed by Fitzwarren. Stove business

Fitzwarren	Well, here we are, alongside of the ship, So far my creditors I've given the slip. But Emmaline, my brain is on the rack, Suppose my creditors are on my track?
Maggie	Ach! Stuff and nonsense! Never backward look. You're not the first to sling yer bloomin' hook.
Fitzwarren	An honest act I'll do, ere Britain's shore I leave, perchance to see it never more.
Maggie	An honest act! Good grief, what might that be?
Fitzwarren	I'll send the landlord of my shop—the key. When I return, no creditors then fighting, I'll vote for better gas and better lighting, Back to back houses, my abomination, I'll even vote for better sanitation. For being in this stoney-broke condition There's one cause only—foreign competition!

Fitzwarren and Maggie exit

Jack enters from one side and Alice from the opposite side

Alice	Yes, this must be the *Betsy Jane*. 'Tis well. But where's the knocker or the street-door bell?
Jack	There stands the proud, pert, pretty little miss; Oh! How I long her ruby lips to kiss! I will! There's no-one here who can assist her. A smack I'll have!

Alice hits Jack on the head with her parasol

Alice	Then you've got one mister!

Jack removes his hat and reveals a huge lump on his head

Jack	I wanted bliss, but she has raised a blister! A blow! Boo-hoo! To scorn I won't be laughed!

He grapples with Alice

Dick enters

Dick Hiya kids!
Audience Hiya Dick!

Part I, Scene 5

Dick espies Jack attacking Alice, and pulls him off

Dick	Avast, you swab! I'm the skipper of this craft!
Alice	Dick!
Dick	Alice!
Alice	Sweetheart!
Dick	Love!
Alice	My life!
Dick	My own!

Maggie enters

Jack   Ha! ha! ha! ha! My power must now be shown!
You seize him, Cookie!

Maggie does so

Cat enters

Maggie	Now we rule the roast.
Jack	And I'll seize her!

The Cat tickles Maggie under the arms, and pulls her cap over her eyes. Maggie: "Aahtchoo!" Audience: "Bless you!" Dick, released, punches Jack on the nose

    Oh great Caesar's Ghost!
Dick   That's how a British sailor serves his foes!
Come on, the lot of you!
Maggie   My eyes!
Dick   My nose!
Jack   Before you hit me again, may I say just one word?
Dick   Yes?
Jack   Help!!!
Maggie   What? Are you frightened of a thing like that?
Jack   All right for you to talk! ... I'll kill that cat!
Alice   Go for them Tom!
Dick   A thrashing now you'll catch.
Yes, Tommy soon will bring them up to scratch.

The Cat has chased Maggie and Jack, and now has them cornered

Alice   To meet you once again indeed is bliss.
Dick   You can't deny me one——
Alice   One what?
Dick   One kiss.
Alice   Oh, well, you must have one, sir, I suppose.
Dick   (*kissing Alice*)   Ah!!
Alice   But please remember that it is sub-rosa!
Maggie   Jack, did you see that?
Jack   Yes ...
Maggie   Then if you're true
Just come and give me a snubnoser too.

Jack	Eh?
Maggie	Don't you believe in the hereafter?
Jack	Of course I believe in the hereafter.
Maggie	Then give us a kiss.
Jack	Why?
Maggie	That's what I'm here-after!

She grabs him in her arms

Fitzwarren, the Captain and Boatswain enter

Fitzwarren	What is ado?
Jack	Why, Dick's a "do", and worse.
Fitzwarren	Dick? What Dick?
Maggie	Why! The Dick who nicked your purse!
Jack	I caught him cuddling Alice.
Captain	The young rake!
Fitzwarren	You've got a nerve, my boy, and no mistake! Come from his side, miss.
Maggie	Here's a cunning ploy. What do you want here?
Dick	I'm the cabin boy!
Maggie	I'll not sail with him.
Alice	Then make up your mind That you are going—to be left behind.
Fitzwarren	The cook must go! I cannot stand sea-cooking.
Captain	P'raps you feel like cancelling your booking?
Fitzwarren	Not my intention, Captain.
Captain	Very well, Then pipe all hands!
Boatswain	Ay! Ay!
Captain	And ring the bell!
Dick	You are the bell(e) I long to "ring".
Alice	You shall Do some day!
Jack	Oh! How I love that gal!
Captain	Now all aboard, and weigh the anchor!
Fitzwarren	Say, What does the anchor generally weigh?
Alice	He means heave up the anchor. You mistake.
Maggie	Don't talk o' heavin', miss, for heevin's sake!
Fitzwarren	Good gracious, Emmaline, don't talk like that.
All	Ahoy! Ahoy! Ahoy!
Jack	I'll kill that cat!

More sailors enter

Song 9

The Captain, Boatswain, Dick, Alice, Maggie, Jack and Fitzwarren sing Song 9 with the company joining in the chorus

Part I, Scene 5

The Stage Manager enters with the words and the audience join in the chorus

Song 10

The Company march on board the "Betsy Jane" during the first chorus. They repeat the chorus, during which the "Betsy Jane" moves off to sea, with the company waving. The image of Queen Vitoria appears on the cyclorama. The company salute

the CURTAIN *falls*

PART II

Scene 6

The Galley of the "Betsy Jane"

A gauze frontcloth scene. There is a table, a long bench and a lantern suspended from above on a straight rod, which at the opening of the scene swings gently from side to side about one foot

 King Rat enters

King Rat That fairy now shall see *my* power! My rats
    Will prove more than a match for twenty cats.
    Holes they have gnawed the vessel's side right through,
    And down she'll go with passengers and crew.

 King Rat exits

The oven gives off a puff of smoke. Audience: "Maggie!"

 Maggie staggers on, carrying an enormous pot which she puts on the table. She staggers over to the stove, which she sees to, then staggers back to the table and lays across it groaning
 Jack enters

Jack What's up? You ill?
Maggie   To come to sea was folly.
    How do *you* feel?
Jack   Particularly jolly!
    'Cos I'm a sailor—no landlubber dunce—
    I sailed from Bermondsey to Blackfriars once.
    The highest waves don't in the least confuse me;
    In fact they only make me feel ... Excuse me!

 Jack rushes out

 Captain and Boatswain enter

Maggie Oh, Captain, stop the barque!
Captain   What's all the fuss?
Maggie I've changed my mind, I think I'll go by bus!
Captain Cheer up ma'am. You'll be better soon, you bet.
Boatswain The old gal hasn't found her sea legs yet.
Maggie Rude sailor! Of you I'll be a wacker!
Boatswain If you're bad ma'am, try a chew o' baccer!

Maggie clasps her hand over her mouth and sits on the bench

Part II, Scene 6

What's this? Supper? (*He rings the bell*) Come-and-get-it! Come-and-get-it!

Dick, Fitzwarren, Jack, the Cat and Alice pile into the galley and head for the table

Dick Hiya kids!
Audience Hiya Dick!
Maggie Just a minute! Just a minute! Have you all washed your hands? Let's have a look at your hands!

They stand in line holding out their hands, Maggie knocks hands down one by one, and they sit on the bench

Right! Right! Right! Right! Right! . . . Aahtchooo! Tommy! Look at those paws! You dirty beast! Go and wash them this minute! Out!

The Cat exits

(*Removing the lid of the pot and drawing out a sock*) Ah, that's where it was! I've been looking for that! (*She dumps a lump of stew on each plate*) Pass it down!

As they pass the plates down the line:

Fitzwarren I say! What is this fly doing in my stew?
Maggie The breast-stroke, I think!
Boatswain I wonder if she's got pigs' trotters?
Jack No, that's just the way she walks!

Maggie hits Jack over the head with her ladle

Captain Order! Order! Order!
Fitzwarren Pardon?
Captain Order!
Jack I'll have a pint!
Maggie You'll get a thick ear in a minute, matie!
Fitzwarren I'm sorry; I can't eat this.
Maggie Why not?
Fitzwarren } (*together*) { I haven't got a spoon!
Others } { He hasn't got a spoon!
Maggie You be quiet.
Captain (*looking into the pot*) Look here, Cook, why have you left the sheep's eyes in this stew?
Others Yes, why have you left the sheep's eyes in this stew?
Maggie So it'll see us through the week!

The lantern swings to the right. They all lean to the left

Alice Look at the lantern!
Jack There's a storm brewing up.

Wind starts, and the ship begins to creak
  Cat enters and joins the others at the table

Fitzwarren Hark at the wind!

The lantern swings to the left, they all lean to the right

Dick The ship's rolling heavily.
Boatswain It's gonna be a rough one!
Captain Sounds like a gale.

The lantern swings to the right, they all swing to the left. Tommy rolls over to the right

Maggie Well come on now, get on with your supper. I want to clear away.

The table slides across to the right side of the stage. (NB: The table is on wheels and can be manœuvred by someone under it, hidden by the tablecloth. It is advisable to have a ridge round the top of the table to prevent plates sliding off. It is so arranged that the bench, also on wheels, slides only to the right side of the stage, and is pushed back into position by the actors. Thus it may be operated by a single line fixed to its base)

Jack Hey!
Boatswain Supper's away!
Maggie Well don't just sit there! Get after it!

Leaning heavily towards the left, they cross to the table, right (like walking down a steep hill). They return the table to its original position (i.e. "uphill")

Captain (*during the above*) Right push!
Boatswain Heave ho!
Maggie All my lovely cooking will be spoilt if it gets cold.
Dick There we are!
Maggie Right! Now let's eat!

They all sit. The lamp swings to the left, they all lean to the right. The table slides to the left side of the stage

Boatswain It's cast off again!
Maggie After it!

Leaning heavily to the right, they cross to the table left, and push it back to centre

Captain Right, push!
Boatswain Heave ho!
Maggie It's not fair. I've stood and cooked this all day.
Dick There we are.
Maggie Now hold it everyone. Hold it!

They all hold the table fast. The lamp swings to the right, they all lean to the left, and the bench slides across to right stage

   Now sit!

They all sit on the floor. They rise and cross to the bench, leaning heavily to the left. They push the bench back to position

Part II, Scene 6

Right, now let's eat!

The lamp swings to the left, they lean to the right, and the table slides to the left. They retrieve the table

Now eat it! Quickly!

Storm Music begins (see page vi)

The lamp swings to the right, they lean to the left, the bench slides to the right side of the stage. They all let go of the table to retrieve the bench. The table slides to the right side of the stage. Alice, Fitzwarren and the Cat retrieve the bench. They sit on it centre stage—Alice in the middle, Fitzwarren and the Cat at either end. Jack, Dick, Captain, Mate and Maggie retrieve the table and bring it to centre

Dick How are you, Alice?
Alice Oh, I do feel poorly.
Gracious, Dick! That was a big wave surely!
Fitzwarren I scarce know what is what, or who is which!
Dick Yes, things have come, sir, to a pretty pitch!
Voice (*off*) Help! Skipper! Help! Help!
Captain Hello, that sounds like trouble. (*To Boatswain and Dick*) You two come with me! The rest carry on!

Captain, Mate, and Dick exit

Jack lets go of the table to salute. Maggie, unable to hold the table on her own, shoots off with it to the right

Maggie Help!

The wind grows louder. Thunder is heard. Fitzwarren and Alice rise and run to help Maggie. The Cat falls off the end of the bench and it rolls to the right. The Cat and Jack push the bench back. Maggie and Alice push the table back. Fitzwarren stands with his fingers in his ears. The thunder stops, the wind lowers, the lamp hangs vertically. The music continues

Jack Ssssh! Can you hear something bumping against the floor?
Fitzwarren Eh?
Jack Under the ship?
Fitzwarren Eh?
Maggie
Alice } (*together*) Under the ship!!
Jack
Fitzwarren Yes, it is. It's an 'orrible trip!
Maggie (*with her ear to the floor*) I wonder what it is!
Jack 'Arf a tick I know the very thing!

Jack exits

Maggie There's something scratchin' and bumpin' about!
Alice Oh, what is it? what is it?

Jack enters with a brace and bit

Jack Now we'll soon find out!

He drills into the deck where Maggie had her ear. A single jet of water springs up

Fitzwarren You fool! You fool! You've sunk us!
Maggie Quick! The stew pot!

Maggie and Alice fetch the stew pot, Jack fetches a mop. They place the stew pot so that it catches the water. (If the jet is at a slight angle, and the pressure gentle but constant, the position is soon found.) Jack mops up whatever spill there may be

Fitzwarren We're sinking! I can feel it!
Maggie Och, look! (*She takes a fish out of the stew pot*) A stow-away!
Fitzwarren We're sinking! We're sinking!

There is a crash of thunder. The Lights fade. The water jet can stop. The lamp swings ad lib. The table, with Maggie and Fitzwarren clinging to it, and the bench with Jack and Alice hanging on, slide ad lib. Tommy somersaults and falls about the deck

> *Through the gauze backcloth we see Captain, Boatswain and Dick aloft, clinging to the mast which swings from side to side with a lighted lantern half-way up it, under an angry sky. The wind howls. There are violent flashes of lightning, and rolls of thunder*

Captain (*yelling*) Take in the topsail!
Voice (*off*) Take in the topsail!
Boatswain LAY HER AHOLD! Ahold!
Voice Ahold!
Captain Bring her to try with the main course!
Boatswain Lay her off! Lay her off!

King Rat enters in a spot downstage

King Rat Blow winds, and crack your cheeks! Rage! Blow!
You cataracts, and hurricanes, spout
Till you have drenched their topsails, drowned the cocks!
You sulphorous and thought executing fires
Singe their mast head. And thou, all shaking thunder
Smite flat the thick rotundity o' the world!
To coin a phrase! ... Ha! Ha! ha! ha! ha! ha!
Captain We split! We split!

The mast crashes to one side

                Abandon ship!

A bell rings

Voice (*off*) Abandon ship!
2nd voice (*off*) Abandon ship!
All Abandon ship!

Part II, Scene 7

Dick rushes into the cabin and takes Alice by the arm, followed by Maggie, Fitzwarren, Jack, and the Cat. They exit. through the gauze we see the Boatswain jump over the side of the ship, followed by the Captain. As Alice Dick, Jack, etc. jump, the Lights begin to fade and there is a final tremendous clap of thunder

Scene 7

Neptune's Palace

Under the sea. In the background we see the wreck of the "Betsy Jane" sink to the bottom. Bubbles. Various cut-out "flown" sea creatures float and swim about

Fish Ballet–Music see page vi

At the end of the ballet Neptune enters and sits on his throne

Neptune Bring in the prisoners!

Two Fish bring in Maggie, Jack, Fitzwarren, Alice and Dick

Dick Hiya kids!
Audience Hiya Dick!
Neptune Silence mortals! Hear report,
Of what you're charged with at my court.
If guilty, we shall waste no time,
The punishment shall fit the crime.
Read the indictment. Make no slips!
1st Fish (*reading*) Eating too much fish and chips!
2nd Fish (*reading*) Eating haddock, eating plaice,
Eating bloaters, cod and dace.
1st Fish Smoking salmon, boiling crabs,
Grilling kippers, frying dabs.
2nd Fish As-salting herrings, making glue
From their bones ground into stew.
1st Fish Boiling lobsters, 'spite their squeals,
Pickling winkles, jellying eels.
2nd Fish Octopus and tadpole drying
Mackerel and tunny frying.
1st Fish Shrimps and prawns and squid and hake,
Perch and roach from out the lake.
2nd Fish Blubber from the whales they boil,
Slaughtering halibut for oil.
1st Fish Sire, the list's as long as that! (*He indicates the scroll*)
The worst offender is their cat!
Neptune Murderers! Tremble you may!
Have you anything to say?
Maggie Well I have to admit, your Warship, I've always been partial to a

nice bit of fish and chips—'specially of a Saturday night. But I never meant anything personal to you!

Neptune Nothing personal to me?
You eat my subjects mercilessly!!!
Jack That was a big help!
Neptune Hear my sentence! Stand and quiver!
You shall be my slaves for ever!
Your cat's escaped, but when he's found,
By my decree he shall be drowned!
Since eating fish is such a lark
I think we'll feed *him* to a shark!
Alice Oh, no! That's wicked! You cruel old man!
Neptune And who are you that you should rail
—Useless mermaid without a tail?
You are all guilty of this slaughter,
So here you stay beneath the water,
With no escape until you're dead.
There's forty fathoms overhead!
Court adjourned!

Neptune and the Fish exit

Maggie Oh, Jack! What are we going to do?
Jack Well, you heard what Moses said—there's forty fathoms of water on top of this cave. We can't get out, we'd all be drowned. We're trapped!
Fitzwarren I never did like the look of that ship.
Maggie Yes, there was something wrong with the mizzen mast.
Fitzwarren What was wrong with the mizzen mast?
Jack It was mizzen!
All We don't wish to know that!
Maggie So we've just come here to die!
Jack No we never, we came here yesterdie!

Maggie thumps him

It's that Tommy's fault!
Maggie It *is* that!
Dick But that's unfair!
Jack I'll kill that cat!
Alice Oh, Dick! I want to go home!
Maggie (*howling*) Me too! I'm home-sick!
Jack But *you* haven't got a home!
Maggie I know. And I'm sick of it!
Fitzwarren Yes, I must admit, it wasn't much of a home, but anything is better than this!
Alice We had such a sweet little garden . . .

Song 11

They all sing Song 11

Maggie } (*together, howling*) We wanna go home!
Jack

Alice But we can't, Jack. We were brought here by magic, and only magic will get us out.

Fairy Bowbells enters

Fairy   Well said, Alice. Do not fear.
               Poor mortals, they can't tell I'm here.
               I won't desert Dick, or his friends,
               And leave them to such watery ends.
               I'll call upon my dear Bowbells,
               And rescue them with fairy spells!

She waves her wand. There is a burst of bubbles, and the sound of bells—muffled by the water

From above a large diving-bell descends. When it reaches the bottom Tommy emerges from the bell. (The bell is a cut-out—Tommy enters via a trap or wing-piece)

Jack Ahhhh! What's that?
Maggie It's the Loch Ness Monster!
Cat Merow!
All It's Tommy!
Maggie Ahhhhtchoooo!
All Bless you!
Dick Quick everyone! Inside!

They all enter the bell, and exit via the trap, or wing-piece. Fairy Bowbells waves her wand, there is a burst of bubbles, and the diving-bell ascends. Fairy Bowbells exits

Neptune enters

Neptune   Now my hearties, work begins!
              Time to expiate your sins!
              What's here? All gone? they won't get far!
              I'll raise a wind from o'er the bar
              Will blow them all to kingdom come
              And liquidate those mortal scum!

Neptune raises his trident, and an ominous rumbling grows louder and louder to a roar, with hissing cymbals, as the Lights fade

SCENE 8

The Coast of Morocco

Jungle noises. A coconut falls on to the stage from above. Monkey swings in on the end of a rope, goes to pick up the coconut, sees the audience, runs to the back of the stage, frightened, looks over his shoulder, comes down to the footlights, peers at the audience—hand over eyes, roars with laughter, waves to the audience, claps and dances about, pointing at the audience with great mirth, stands on his head, stands up again, hears someone coming, looks off, swings off with coconut under his arm

Princess Jujube enters to sing:

Song 12

The last chorus is repeated with the audience

Unnoticed by Jujube, four Rats enter and dance a mock can-can behind her. At the end of the chorus Jujube sees them, and runs off screaming, chased by Rats

Sultan Rustifustican, Zeldomphed and two Guards enter. Rustifustican wears an enormous ornate turban

Rustifustican Zeldomphed!
Zeldomphed Yes, your serenity.
Rustifustican Have you hung out the what-you-call-'ems on the thingamies?
Zeldomphed Precisely, O Pertinacity!
Rustifustican And posted the thingumebobs on the what's-its-name?
Zeldomphed Indubitably, ubiquity.
Rustifustican Then read us the you-know-what!
Zeldomphed (*reading*) "Know, all men, by these presents———"
Rustifustican "Presents?" What presents?
Zeldomphed We will come to that presently, your serenity—"that whereas this our land is overrun with rats—to him who can rid us of these devastating pests will be given in marriage our royal daughter's hand, and half of our unknown wealth. Rustifustican, the Ninetyouth".
Rustifustican Any applicants yet?
Zeldomphed None, your supremity.
Rustifustican Why not? Why not?

Jujube rushes in

Jujube	The rats! The rats! They're nibbling our toeses!
Rustifustican	Allah preserve us! They'll soon be at our noses!
Jujube	How to get rid of them, that's the burning question.
Rustifustican	Feed 'em on cake till they get indigestion!
Jujube	They haven't left a bit of cake. Not one.
Rustifustican	What! Taken all the cake? They take the bun!
	But leave us now. Alone I may determine
	Upon a plan to rid us of these vermin.
	(*To Guards*) Eyes front! my Calton Swaddies.
	Right about—Face! Quick march! or otherwise—
	—get out!

Jujube, Zeldomphed and the Guards exit

> Could only some all powerful God
> Exterminate the rat,

> I'd fast a fortnight, sleep on nails,
> I'd even eat my hat!

Song 13

Rustifustican sings Song 13

The Stage Manager wheels on the words for the audience to join in

Rustifustican exits

The stove gives off a puff of smoke and the audience shouts: "Maggie!"

Maggie enters wearing only her underwear and a barrel

Maggie Well, here I am, the only survivor! But *where* am I? It's a queer place this and no mistake—there's not a sewer in sight! That storm blew us all up on the rocks, and now me feet are killing me. And I'm that hungry! I'm starvin'. I used to be a bonnie lassie, now I'm just a boney chassis! (*Howling*) What am I going to do for food?!!

A coconut falls from above and hits her on the head

What was that? Hit me right on me birthmark! Have you seen my birthmark? I got it climbin' into the wrong berth! But where did that *come* from! All I said was ... (*she howls*) What am I going to do for food?!!

A shower of coconuts descends from above

That'll do! That'll do! I've not finished the first course yet! (*She grabs a coconut and bangs it on the ground, trying to open it*)

The Monkey swings in on his rope, and stands behind Maggie, and hits her on the head with another coconut—What was it? Where is he? Oh no he isn't! etc., business with audience

(*Offering her hand*) Er ... how do you do?

Monkey takes her hand, pulls her on to her stomach—still wearing her barrel—and spins her round and round

Native Guards, followed by Rustifustican enter. The Guards bring her to her feet

Monkey runs off

Rustifustican Oh, vision of loveliness!
Maggie (*aside*) A man! I wonder if I'm all right behind?
Rustifustican (*aside*) If this were India she'd be sacred! I'll mash her, and if she's a failure as a wife, she'll always come in handy for the larder! (*Aloud*) Whence come you madam?
Maggie From the sea, and ...
Rustifustican Ah, then you are a mermaid!
Maggie Well you're a mere man, but I'm willing to make allowances!
Rustifustican Not at all, madam. I am a potentate!
Maggie Oh, you poor fellow! That can be very painful!

Rustifustican (*aside*) The trouble is with white-women—they're delicious at the time, but in half an hour you're hungry all over again! (*Aloud*) I am an emperor, madam!

Maggie (*aside*) Oooh! Here's me chance to be an empress! I'll impress him with me Sloane Street smile!

Rustifustican What are you doing?

Maggie I'm smiling!

Rustifustican Can't you take something for it? What is your front name?

Maggie Emmaline.

Rustifustican Then Emma lean your head upon our royal chest.

Maggie Why?

Rustifustican We want you for one of our wives!

Maggie *One* of your wives? *One* of your wives? How many wives have you got?

Rustifustican Same as Englishman—sixteen!

Maggie There's no Englishman with sixteen wives!

Rustifustican Me read in Bible—four better—four worse—four richer—four poorer. Sixteen! Come! You can join worse! (*As they all exit*) I'm afraid the larder has it!

All exit

Jujube enters with Jack over her shoulder

Jujube Hey, papa! Look what I found, Papa!

She stands Jack down

Jack (*dazedly*) Well, here I am, the only survivor. Where am I?

Jujube Me find you on the beach, white boy. You're mine!

Jack ... Cor!

Jujube You very brown for a white boy. Sunburn?

Jack No—rust! I wonder what happened to Cookie. You seen our Cookie?

Jujube You mean the mermaid?

Jack If I do, it's the wrong end of the fish.

Jujube My papa carry her off to the palace.

Jack Ah well, there goes my meal ticket—just my luck.

Jujube Yarooooo!

She flings him over her shoulder and exits

Fitzwarren and Alice enter

Fitzwarren Well, here we are Alice, the only survivors!

Alice Perhaps the others are safe too, Papa. You never know.

Fitzwarren Phoo! Let's rest a bit, my dear. I'm not as young as I was. I suppose you're worried about young Whittington.

Alice Yes, Papa.

Fitzwarren And if you find him again, I suppose you two will be off together—no time for your poor old father then.

Alice Papa! How can you say such a thing. I shall never leave you like that.

Part II, Scene 8   39

Fitzwarren That's what you say now, my dear, but later on . . .
Alice You know that's not true!

Song 14

Fitzwarren and Alice sing Song 14

   The Stage Manager wheels on the words of the chorus for the audience to join in

   Alice and Fitzwarren exit

   Dick and the Cat enter

Dick Hiya kids!
Audience Hiya Dick!
Dick Well, here we are Tommy—the only survivors!
Cat Merow!
Dick I only hope the natives are friendly. Hello! What's this?—A clearing sale? (*He reads the Sultan's proclamation*) "Rats?" "Princess?" "Fortune?" Tommy, the prize is ours!
Cat Merow!

   Zeldomphed enters with Guards who seize Dick and Cat

Zeldomphed Seize them! . . . Who are you?
Dick We're British subjects, and in Britain's name
Your hospitality we humbly claim.
Zeldomphed Young man we'll do the best we can for you
If you've any f-u-d—food! with you.
Dick Food! Lor' we're starving!
Zeldomphed I must make admission
That all the court are in the same condition.
A plague of——
Dick ⎫
Zeldomphed ⎬ (*together*)   Rats!
Zeldomphed Correct! But rather rude—
Has left our land without a bit of food.
Dick Then now your worry's over!
Zeldomphed How is that?
Dick Tommy here shall vanquish every rat.
Zeldomphed Then to the palace come, at once, away!
We'll put him to the test without delay.
If he succeeds you're wealthy.
Dick If he fails?
Zeldomphed Your head shall pay the forfeit of your tales.

   As they all exit a coconut drops on to the stage

Tommy stays behind to investigate

   Monkey swings on beside Tommy

They look at each other curiously for a moment. Then they creep towards each other, and sniff each other. Tommy does a somersault. Monkey does a somersault. Monkey stands on his head. Tommy tries to copy him but falls over. Monkey laughs. They circle round—eyeing each other. Tommy taps his foot three times, Monkey copies him. (Music: chorus of "Lily Of Laguna") Tommy taps his other foot three times, Monkey copies him. Tommy starts to dance a soft-shoe-shuffle. Monkey joins him, and they dance together

At the end of the dance, they exit

Scene 9

The Sultan's Palace

Rustifustican is seated with his court and guests on cushions. Harem girls are dancing

Maggie enters in a bizarre eastern costume, clutching a guitar. She serenades Rustifustican, à la Scheherazade. (Music—see page vi) Maggie plucks the two recurring notes on her guitar—"Plonk-plonk!" She joins and leads the dancing

Song 15

Rustifustican sings Song 15

The Stage Manager wheels on the chorus words for the audience to join in

Maggie and the girls dance off

Rustifustican (*to Jack*) I'm afraid, my young friend, I robbed you.
Jack Not at all Sultan, not at all.
Rustifustican Do call me Jim. I'm afraid you'll miss her.
Jack Well never mind Jim, I expect you'll throw in a consolation stake, eh?
Rustifustican Have her back, my boy, have her back! You shall have her back at cost price. Damme, you shall have her as a gift.
Jack Not even as a gift old pard', I've already taken up with quite a different package!

The stove gives off a big puff of smoke. The audience shout "Maggie!"

Maggie enters, and crosses to the stove

Maggie Ah, the wedding breakfast! It should just about be ready. Just as promised!
Rustifustican Ah, food at last!

Everyone rises in expectation. Maggie takes the turkey from the oven, now done nice and brown, and carries it to the barren wedding table

Maggie Oh yes! Yes! Look at that! Thank you, children! It's the children that did it, you know, they looked after it for me. Give 'em a round of applause!

Part II, Scene 9

The cast clap the audience

The stage is invaded by Rats, who swarm over the table, grab the turkey, and squabble over it centre stage

The ladies scream in horror

King Rat enters

King Rat   Aha! my beauties, having fun?

One of the Rats runs off with the turkey, hotly pursued by the other Rats

> At last my victory's begun!
> Soon this island will be mine,
> And when I've done for you poor swine,
> And all my armies are unfurled,
> I'll soon be ruler of the world.
> Dick Whittington, you feeble sap,
> You sailed right in my cunning trap.
> My thirst for vengeance won't be sated
> Till I'm sure you're liquidated!

He draws his sword and approaches the unarmed Dick. The others cower away in terror

There is a violent squealing from the rats off-stage. They enter and rush across the stage in panic, followed by Tommy in hot pursuit

Maggie sneezes "Aaatchooo!" Tommy and King Rat circle each other, snarling. King Rat strikes at Tommy with his sword, but Tommy dodges. Dick snatches a sword from one of the guards, and throws it to Tommy who catches it. Tommy and King Rat fight. Finally Tommy runs King Rat through

King Rat drags himself off, mortally wounded. Tommy runs after him
The others watch the coup de grâce off-stage

Tommy returns with a small model of King Rat, which he lays at Rustifustican's feet

Rustifustican   Oh wond'rous cat, to overcome such odds!
Kneel my subjects, he must be from the Gods!

Rustifustican, Jujube, Zeldomphed and the rest of the Sultan's court kneel. Rustifustican pulls Maggie down and Jujube makes Jack kneel

Dick   Well done, Tommy!
Zeldomphed   How he on them did fall!
Alice   How large they were!
                        Well, Tom soon made them small!
Rustifustican   Your promise you have kept, and now behold,
Thy rich reward, ten sacks of glitt'ring gold.

The Guards produce the sacks of gold

Jujube   The prize is worth the winning friends?

All	Oh! yes!!
Alice	Sacks upon sacks of gold!
Zeldomphed	And a princess!
Dick	But I don't want a princess!
Rustifustican	What, sir?
Zeldomphed	Well!
Dick	I promised long ago to ring this bell(e).
Rustifustican	Refuse the princess!
Zeldomphed	No-one could be nicer.
Jack	It's all right, Jimmy, I intend to splice her.
Maggie	What's that?!
Fitzwarren	Now Maggie dear, don't make a fuss. What's good for them is just as good for *us*!
Maggie	Oooh, Fitzy! You've made me come over all unnecessary! You devil! (*She buries her head in his shoulder*)

Bells, very distant

Dick	For London, ho!
Alice	Wherever we may roam, As the song says, "There's not place like home!"

Song 16

Dick and Company sing Song 16

As the Lights fade to Black-out Fairy Bowbells enters lit only in her spot

Fairy	Though Dick's triumph is at hand, Let's first return to Fairyland, Where friends of Harlequin await To hear his story, or his fate. He too will have a big surprise, Will Harlequin believe *his* eyes?

Scene 10

The Land of Fancy: Harlequinade

Fairy Bowbells, Columbine, Pantaloon, Butcher and the Watchman are playing Blindman's Buff. On the floor is Clown's poker. Pantaloon is blindfolded and is reaching out for the others. He takes hold of Fairy Bowbells' wand. It gives him an electric shock. The others laugh. He catches Butcher, who is then blindfolded and turned three times. He catches Columbine. He touches her face and shoulders, then seizes her in his arms and tries to kiss her. Pantaloon takes hold of Butcher, and the Watchman takes hold of Pantaloon as they try to pull Butcher off

Tommy the Cat springs on carrying Harlequin's bat

He strikes Butcher's hands. Butcher lets go, and he, Pantaloon and Watchman fall down. They rise and back away from the Cat in wonder. Fairy Bowbells waves her wand. There is a flash and Cat is transformed back into Harlequin. Harlequin and Columbine embrace. A coconut flies on from the wings and hits Pantaloon

Monkey enters

The others are astonished. Harlequin takes Monkey by the hand and introduces him. They all shake hands. Monkey stands on his head. Harlequin and Monkey do a bit of their soft-shoe-shuffle. The others applaud. Harlequin spies Clown's poker, and looks round. Where is Clown? The others laugh and shrug their shoulders. What is the joke—demands Harlequin. Fairy Bowbells steps in and waves her wand. There is another flash, and Monkey is changed back into Clown! You!—says Harlequin, it was you, all the time! Clown nods. They all laugh. Harlequin and Clown do their soft-shoe shuffle together again. This time all the others join in

They dance off

Wedding bells

Fairy   And so to London's Guildhall, we
Must witness Dick make history.
"Three times Lord Mayor" the bells do ring,
And yet of other triumphs sing—
Society in best array
At Dick and Alice's Wedding Day!

SCENE 11

Finale, and walk-down

The Guildhall, London

Music. Dick with his bride Alice, are discovered at the foot of a magnificent staircase

Dick Hiya kids
Audience Hiya Dick!
Dick   Most welcome guests!
Alice   Yes, welcome all of you!
For all have prov'd themselves staunch friends and true!
Dick   Of their fond worth let's show our admiration,
And greet their tributes with a warm ovation.

The company enter, group by group, to the top of the stairs, descend, bow to Dick and Alice, come downstage and bow to the audience, and line up either side of the stage. When Tommy bows penultimately (before Dick and Alice finally take their bow to the audience) Maggie sneezes: "Aaatchooo!"

All Bless you!
Fitzwarren   All's ended well for us 'tis very true,

	But has it also ended well for you? (*To the audience*)
Jujube	What signify Dick's riches, fame and glory,
	If you—our patrons—relish not our story?
Rustifustican	Alice's favour, Whittington secures,
	And we won't grumble if we share in yours.
Maggie	I hope you find our dish of fun all right,
	Not overdone, but pleasant—rich, yet light—
	And such as you can recommend to any;
	A dish not spoiled by just one cook too many!
Jack	They call me Idle Jack, now is that true—
	Have I been idle? I appeal to you!
Alice	Our tale is told. Be lenient with our rhyme,
	'Tis not a poem but a Pantomime—
	A harmless piece of Christmas jingling folly
	To help poor mortals banish melancholy.
Dick	To gain this end your humble friends have striven,
	I trust that satisfaction we have given,
	And Pantomime has once more done the trick.
	I wish you well, and—Cheerio kids!
All	Cheerio Dick!

Reprise of Song 16

The Company sing the reprise

The Stage Manager wheels on the words for the audience

CURTAIN

FURNITURE AND PROPERTY LIST

PART I

SCENE 1

On stage: Milestone behind gauze curtain

Personal: **Fairy Bowbells:** wand (used throughout)
Harlequin: magic bat
Clown: poker
Dick: bag or pack containing bread

SCENE 2

On stage: Water pump
Table (collapsible)

Off stage: Words of Song 1 chorus on easel **(Stage Manager)**
Burning black pie **(Maggie)**
Victorian gas-stove with turkey on top **(Stage Manager)** *NB: stove remains onstage for rest of performance*
Words of Song 3 chorus on easel **(Stage Manager)**

SCENE 3

On stage: Counter. *On it:* food remains, bags, jars of sweets. *Behind it:* blue braces, bottle of aspirin, **Dick's** bag containing **Fitzwarren's** purse
Shelves. *On them:* jars of sweets, bottles of drink
Cash desk. *On it:* till
Ladder
Bell on shop door

Behind gauze: table with empty bottle on it, chair

Off stage: Bottle gin **(Urchin)**

Personal: **Children, customers:** money
Bailiff: eviction order
Fitzwarren: penny

SCENE 4

On stage: Milestone

Off stage: Words of Song 6 chorus on easel **(Stage Manager)**
"Snow" **(Snowflakes)**

Personal: **Dick:** bag, penny

Scene 5

On stage: Cut-out of the *Betsy Jane*
Barrel. *On it:* book, pen
2 notices, as per script

Off stage: Large crate **(Captain** and **Boatswain)**
Words of Song 8 chorus on easel **(Stage Manager)**
Words of Song 9 chorus on easel **(Stage Manager)**
Words of Song 10 on easel **(Stage Manager)**

Personal: **Dick:** bag
Alice: parasol
Jack: bump on head

Scene 6

On stage: Table. *On it:* tablecloth, plates, ladle
Bench
Lantern suspended on straight rod
Bell
Mop

Behind gauze: mast with lighted lantern

Off stage: Enormous pot containing sock, stew and fish **(Maggie)**
Brace and bit **(Jack)**

PART II

Set: Cooked turkey in stove for Scene 9

Scene 7

On stage: Throne
Cut-outs of sea creatures

Off stage: Wreck of the *Betsy Jane* **(Stage Management)**
2 scrolls **(1st** and **2nd Fish)**
Diving-bell **(Stage Management)**

Personal: **Neptune:** trident

Scene 8

On stage: Trees. *On one:* proclamation

Off stage: Rope for **Monkey**
Coconut **(Stage Management)**
Scroll **(Zeldomphed)**
Words of Song 13 chorus on easel **(Stage Manager)**
Coconut **(Stage Management)**
Shower of coconuts **(Stage Management)**
Rope, coconut **(Monkey)**
Words of Song 14 chorus on easel **(Stage Manager)**
Coconut **(Stage Management)**

Dick Whittington

	Rope **(Monkey)**
Personal:	**Maggie:** barrel

SCENE 9

On stage:	Cushions Table
Off stage:	Guitar **(Maggie)** Words of Song 15 chorus on easel **(Stage Manager)** Model of King Rat **(Tommy the Cat)** Sacks of gold **(Guards)**
Personal:	**King Rat:** sword **Guards:** swords

SCENE 10

On stage:	**Clown**'s poker
Off stage:	**Harlequin**'s bat **(Tommy)** Coconuts **(Stage Management)**
Personal:	**Pantaloon:** blindfold

SCENE 11

On stage:	Nil
Off stage:	Words of Song 17 on easel **(Stage Management)**

LIGHTING PLOT

Property fittings required: 2 ship's lanterns

Various interior and exterior settings

PART I, SCENE 1

To open: Spot on **Fairy Bowbells**

Cue 1	**Fairy:** "... our Christmas holiday ..." *Bring up lights on Harlequinade characters*	(Page 1)
Cue 2	**Fairy** exits *Cut spot*	(Page 1)
Cue 3	**Fairy:** "Then just behold!" *Bring up lights behind gauze to reveal* **Dick**	(Page 4)
Cue 4	**Dick** and **Cat** move off together *Fade lights behind gauze*	(Page 4)

PART I, SCENE 2

To open: General exterior lighting

No cues

PART I, SCENE 3

To open: General interior lighting

Cue 5	During second chorus of Song 5 *Bring up lights behind gauze to reveal The Drunkard's House*	(Page 16)
Cue 6	At end of Song 5 *Fade lights behind gauze*	(Page 16)

PART I, SCENE 4

To open: General exterior lighting

Cue 7	**Jack Frost** appears *Lights become hard and cold*	(Page 19)
Cue 8	**Jack Frost** summons up wind and snow *Snow-lighting effect*	(Page 20)
Cue 9	**Sunbeams** enter, dancing *Slowly change to warm, sunny lighting with rosy dawn glow at one side*	(Page 20)

Dick Whittington

PART I, Scene 5

To open: General exterior lighting

Cue 10	As *Betsy Jane* moves off with cast *Image of Queen Victoria on sky at back*	(Page 27)

PART II, Scene 6

To open: General interior lighting, lantern lit

Cue 11	**Fitzwarren:** "We're sinking! We're sinking!" *Lights fade; bring up lighting behind gauze to reveal mast with lighted lantern; flashes of lighting*	(Page 32)
Cue 12	**King Rat** enters *Spot on him downstage*	(Page 32)
Cue 13	As **Alice, Dick, Jack,** etc. jump *Fade lights*	(Page 33)

PART II, Scene 7

To open: Underwater lighting

Cue 14	Ominous rumbling grows louder to a roar *Fade lights*	(Page 35)

PART II, Scene 8

To open: Warm, sunny exterior lighting

No cues

PART II, Scene 9

To open: General interior lighting

Cue 15	At end of second chorus of Song 16 *Fade lights to black-out; bring up spot on* **Fairy**	(Page 42)

PART II, Scene 10

To open: General lighting for Harlequinade

No cues

PART II, Scene 11

To open: Bright, general lighting

No cues

EFFECTS PLOT

PART I

Cue 1	**Fairy** touches **Harlequin** with her wand *Flash, puff of smoke*	(Page 3)
Cue 2	**Fitzwarren** chases **Jack** off *Loud explosion from inside house*	(Page 6)
Cue 3	**Maggie:** "... better than that ..." *Puff of smoke from stove*	(Page 7)
Cue 4	**Maggie:** "... I'm that grateful, children ..." *Repeat Cue 3*	(Page 7)
Cue 5	**Maggie** grabs **Jack** into her arms *Repeat Cue 3*	(Page 8)
Cue 6	After last chorus of Song 3 *Repeat Cue 3*	(Page 10)
Cue 7	**Rat** returns and approaches stove *Repeat Cue 3*	(Page 12)
Cue 8	As SCENE 4 opens *Bells ringing in distance*	(Page 18)
Cue 9	**King Rat:** "... *freeze* this stupid pair!" *Hissing and crash of cymbals*	(Page 19)
Cue 10	**Jack Frost** summons up wind and snow *Icy wind and snow effect*	(Page 20)
Cue 11	As lighting becomes sunny and warm *Fade wind and snow effect; birdsong*	(Page 20)
Cue 12	**Fairy:** "Peal out, ye merry bells ..." *Bells ring*	(Page 20)
Cue 13	**Voices** (*off; crescendo*): "London's Lord Mayor!" *Bells swell in a crescendo; fade as* SCENE 5 *begins*	(Page 21)
Cue 14	**All** exit *Puff of smoke from stove*	(Page 24)

PART II

Cue 15	At opening of SCENE 6 *Lantern swings gently from side to side—continue*	(Page 28)
Cue 16	**King Rat** exits *Puff of smoke from stove*	(Page 28)

Cue 17	**Maggie:** "... see us through the week!" *Lantern swings to right*	(Page 29)
Cue 18	**Jack:** "... a storm brewing up." *Wind starts, ship begins to creak*	(Page 29)
Cue 10	**Fitzwarren:** "Hark at the wind!" *Lantern swings to left*	(Page 30)
Cue 20	**Captain:** "Sounds like a gale." *Lantern swings to right*	(Page 30)
Cue 21	They all sit *Lantern swings to left*	(Page 30)
Cue 22	They all hold the table fast *Lantern swings to right, bench slides across to right*	(Page 30)
Cue 23	**Maggie:** "... now let's eat!" *Lantern swings to left*	(Page 31)
Cue 24	**Maggie:** "Now eat it! Quickly!" *Lantern swings to right, bench slides to right*	(Page 31)
Cue 25	**Maggie:** "Help!" *Wind increases, thunder*	(Page 31)
Cue 26	**Cat** falls off end of bench *Bench rolls to right*	(Page 31)
Cue 27	**Fitzwarren** stands with fingers in his ears *Stop thunder, lower wind; lantern hangs vertically*	(Page 31)
Cue 28	**Jack** drills into deck *Jet of water*	(Page 32)
Cue 29	**Fitzwarren:** "We're sinking! We're sinking!" *Crash of thunder; stop water jet; lantern swings ad lib, also bench; wind howls, rolls of thunder*	(Page 32)
Cue 30	**Captain:** "We split! We split!" *Crash as mast falls to one side*	(Page 32)
Cue 31	**Captain:** "Abandon ship!" *Bell rings*	(Page 32)
Cue 32	As **Alice, Dick, Jack,** etc. jump *Tremendous final clap of thunder*	(Page 33)
Cue 33	As SCENE 7 opens *Bubbles as wreck of the "Betsy Jane" sinks to bottom*	(Page 33)
Cue 34	As **Fairy** waves her wand *Burst of bubbles as diving-bell descends; muffled bells*	(Page 35)
Cue 35	**All** enter bell; **Fairy** waves her wand *Burst of bubbles as bell ascends*	(Page 35)
Cue 36	**Neptune** raises his trident *Ominous rumbling, growing louder to a roar, with hissing cymbals*	(Page 35)

Cue 37	As Scene 8 opens *Jungle noises*	(Page 35)
Cue 38	**Rustifustican** exits *Puff of smoke from stove*	(Page 37)
Cue 39	**Jack:** "... different package!" *Big puff of smoke from stove*	(Page 40)
Cue 40	**Maggie:** "You devil!" *Bells, very distant*	(Page 42)
Cue 41	**Fairy** waves her wand *Flash*	(Page 43)
Cue 42	**Fairy** waves her wand *Flash*	(Page 43)
Cue 43	Harlequinade characters dance off *Wedding bells*	(Page 43)

MADE AND PRINTED IN GREAT BRITAIN BY
LATIMER TREND & COMPANY LTD PLYMOUTH
MADE IN ENGLAND

www.ingramcontent.com/pod-product-compliance
Ingram Content Group UK Ltd.
Pitfield, Milton Keynes, MK11 3LW, UK
UKHW021847210426
5322IPUK00022B/522